Prime

poems by

Miranda Pearson

Porcepic Books
an imprint of

Beach Holme Publishing
Vancouver

First Edition

This book is published by Beach Holme Publishing, 226-2040 West 12th Avenue, Vancouver, B.C. V6J 2G2. *www.beachholme.bc.ca.* This is a Porcepic Book.

The publisher gratefully acknowledges the financial support of the Canada Council for the Arts and of the British Columbia Arts Council. The publisher also acknowledges the financial assistance received from the Government of Canada through the Book Publishing Industry Development Program (BPIDP) for its publishing activities.

Editor: Michael Carroll
Production and Design: Jen Hamilton
Cover Art: Angela Grossmann, copyright © 2000. Used with the permission of the artist.
Author Photograph: Christopher Morris

Printed and bound in Canada by Marc Veilleux Imprimeur

National Library of Canada Cataloguing in Publication Data

Pearson, Miranda.
Prime

Poems.
"A Porcepic book."
ISBN 0-88878-418-X

I. Title.
PS8581.E388P7 2001 C811'.54 C2001-910122-8
PR9199.3.P373P7 2001

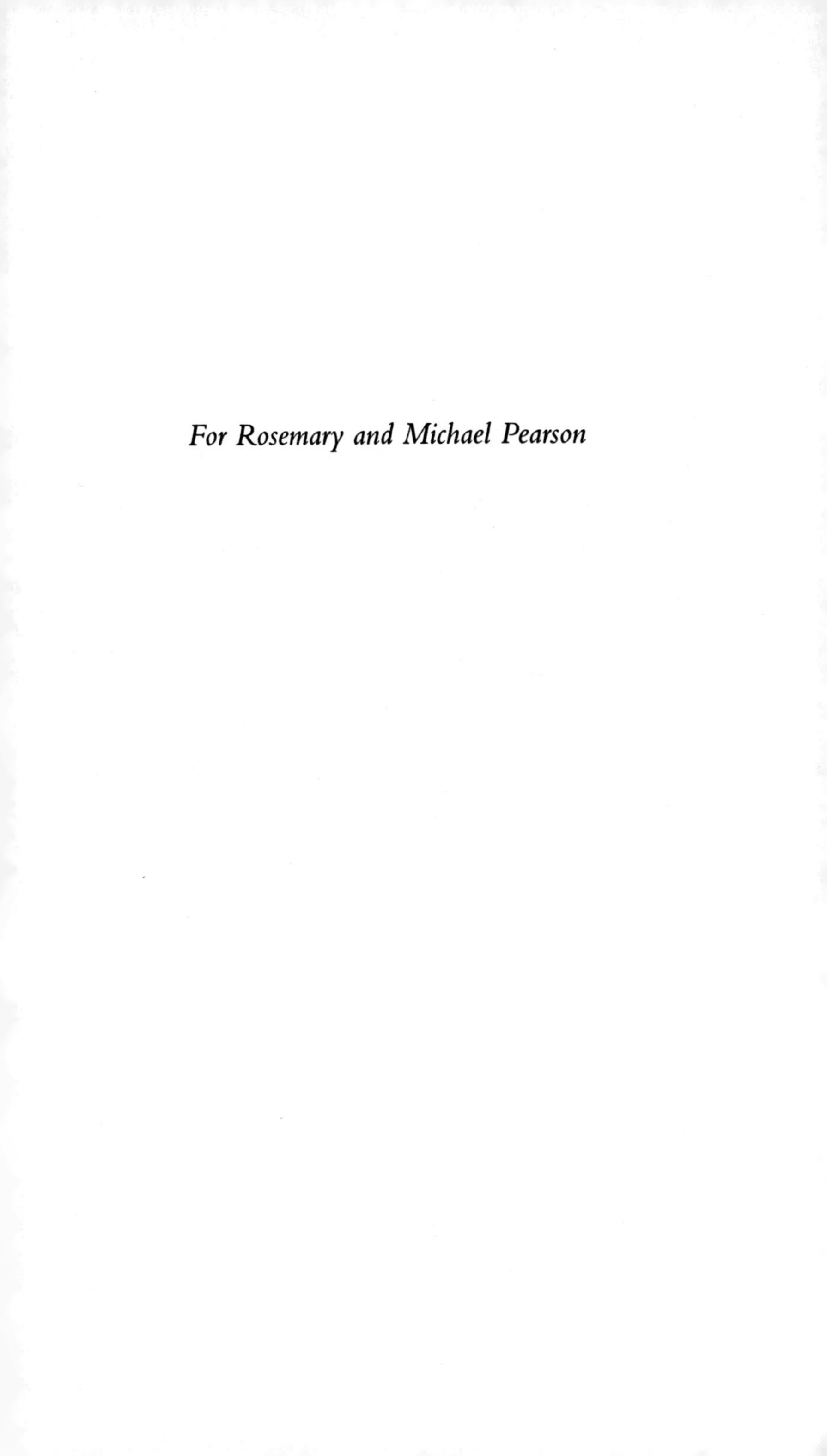

For Rosemary and Michael Pearson

Contents

Acknowledgements

For their close editorial attention to this book, I would like to thank: Don McKay and the Sage Hill Poetry Colloquium; Mark Cochrane, Esta Spalding, and Roo Borson; George McWhirter and the University of British Columbia M.F.A. Advanced Poetry Workshop.

And for their suggestions and encouragement, thanks go to Patrick Lane, Di Brandt, Marilyn Dumont, Kate Braid, Denise Ryan, Monica Franz, Shawna Fowler, Souix Browning, Tanis Macdonald, Katherine Kerr, John Barton, Steven Herrick, Richard Harrison, Kathleen Jamie, Joy Gugeler, Patricia Young, Julie Bruck, Janice Kulyk-Keefer, and Rhonda Batchelor at Reference West.

Sincere gratitude is also extended to Tracey Dobney and all at Vista; to Gillian Cornford, Carola Ackery, Mark Harris, and Andrew Currie; and to Adam Pearson-Currie.

Many thanks to Angela Grossmann for the cover art; to Christopher Morris for the author photo; and to Michael Carroll, Jen Hamilton, and Trisha Telep at Beach Holme.

Earlier versions of several of these poems were first published in the following literary journals: *The Antigonish Review, Arc, Canadian Literature, Event, The Fiddlehead, Grain, The Malahat Review, Matrix, Prairie Fire, Prism international, TADs 6,* and *Wascana Review.* My thanks to the editors.

Poems from this book also appear in the limited-edition chapbook *After the Body* (Reference West, 1996). "The Measure," "Off Jericho," and "Greenham" are in the anthology *At the Edges of Time* (Seraphim, 2000, ed. Maureen Whyte).

Finally, love and thanks to Mark.

One

Falling in Love

I am falling in love
with myself

I lie in the bath
hilly as a Henry Moore
and I admire   I
admire
the sheen of my skin
stretched as eggshell
over my belly
the parcel
the big egg

I am falling in love
with my silver shoulders
as they support these breasts
blue-laced
floating
like swollen planets
        I hardly recognize them
        they have become
        so
        useful

I am falling in love
with my stranded body
stupefied
by pregnancy

in empathy
with the old and obese

I have always suspected
this was my true self
emerging
from hesitant bones
    queen-sized
    and undisguised
    by vanity

Dinner with Friends on a Midsummer's Evening

Angela's lime-green parrot shuffles,
long tail a straight blade.

Our dresses, blood-orange, white, African-striped,
our big bare suntanned shoulders and
flowery names: *Carola, Gillie, Angela, Miranda,*
we pat each other, tell each other we look great,
you've lost weight
no, I wish
no, really

The petunias on the table frame her,
gauzy shells dipped in pink watercolour;
they will only last a night.
We pass around the red sauce,
the black olives, the wine,
the flowers.
I try not to look at her breasts as she talks.

We get stuck talking men, lost loves,
pregnancies welcomed and not,
the crazy conviction of lust
that we followed
as if our lives depended on it,

and perhaps it was
the only door we could see through back then,
the track away from home,
a dodgy compass, its guessing finger.
The talk flows but keeps coming back to
love, a lake that empties,

revealing the slimy wrecks of trucks,
the cracked earth,
then the next time you look
it's full again, beckoning swimmers.

Drunk, I say:
it's women who have always meant more to me,
and there's a pause.

The parrot is walking on the table.

Angela leans toward me
a distraction of dark cleavage,
her painter's hands raised and imploring,
her lipstick smeared, and says
oh, but it's the difference
that's so interesting,

and I agree,
because by then
I would have said *yes*
to anything.

Off Jericho

we swam,
bobbing seal heads in the sea, daring to
push out farther, till we were
black beads to the lifeguards, their raised binoculars.
Our children, engrossed in the
swarming particulars of seashore, lifted bright armfuls
of spinachy seaweed, watched by reluctant friends
who hadn't realized we would be gone long, but
so far we swam, the beach kneeled
into the drifting body of sea, it rose up to be
a pewter shelf. We delayed there, trod water.
This was the best time: the mountains across the bay
sat grand in their crumpled ball gowns, and we beneath,
as if children, twin heads, pearly legs kicking
past old fears of biting fish, red tide, pollution, out
where the freighters graze, remembering China.

Blended

Smile.
Do not stutter or wring your hands.
This cup is half full, tell them, this ink blot
a ballerina, a rising sun.
There are no monsters here,
this is a house to *envy*. Do not

hesitate, even when you wake
full of vertigo from dreaming
your house has again been robbed
the rooms empty, white
squares on the walls
where the paintings used to hang.

Above all, convince the children you
are glad, that you designed
the patchwork quilt
with absolute purpose.

Be sure the kitchen smells of baking;
give them each a wooden spoon
and let them fold the cake.
            Explain the cracking of eggs.

Lead them into the new garden,
plant seeds together
in the earth you have turned,
            watch for green.

And if you have to, talk big
like a TV wrestler.
Face the camera and scare yourself

with your snarling lip
your beetle eyes
your bronzed, shining body.

Lengths

In the bright glass
geometry of the swimming pool
we crawl through our muffled worlds,
masked, half-blind, bodies sailing but so
intimate, bumper to bumper.
My hand licks skin—a second
of unerotic miscalculation,
we're all practically naked but we stay
in our *own lanes.*

Under trembling cracked water
the stranger's skin is magnified
white and pickled in laboratory blue,
revealing the goose bumps that prove
we're not far off reptilian,
earnestly floundering back
to our primitive selves, but careful
not to touch.

Between Your Parents' Sheets

After the beach we rinse off sand into your parents'
swimming pool, our hair drips chlorine in the elevator
up to the twenty-second floor.
In their hushed apartment I weigh myself
against your mother's scales. There's no hiding here,
so high and bright, birds fly below
and the city is a film unrolling.

The telescope boys are surely out today,
zooming in on us; our matched bodies
flop onto your parents' bed, breaking its seal,
the room anonymous and humming as a hotel room,
floating, locked in its outsized windows,
the sum of traffic working itself out below.

A black hair on the pillow—your father's?
Lilacs open in odourless reproduction in the
print above the bed and I feel I *am* your mother
as I stretch out on her side, my body
only a few years younger than hers
and less well toned. What are you thinking?

You told me my mouth is like hers.
I have watched it closing
on glasses of white wine.
Your buttocks are white as you peel off
your bathing suit in the murky
closed eye of the TV, its

friendly angle at the foot of the bed
reflecting my shins at shiny angles around you.
We fuck as *they* must fuck. Disguised
in your father's body you at last
take his shape—and no one stops you.

Party

for Dill

My mother, beautiful in shocking
pink, pearls piled round her neck,
sways through the party, cigarette holder
aloft like a wand.

A few martinis and they were all stars,
lipstick smears on the men's flushed cheeks,
bottles foaming into raised glasses.
Canapés jewelled on trays held high
above the loud crowd.

We watched through the banisters,
our flammable nighties static with electricity,
pointing out the grown-ups, discussing
who loved who:
Mrs. Martin kissed Mr. Smith
that means she'll marry him now.

Uncertain of details we bounced on beds,
pitched by the laughter and music below.
Slipped downstairs into the summer night, the cool
of lilac and dew.

We climbed on the cars while the party flared, pink
and orange windows flickering with cutouts,
we sang our favourite song:
I don't care what you say
I won't stay in a world
Without love.

Eight-year-old divas on the VWs and Rovers,
pounding up and down
to test the bendability of the metal
and singing as if backed by a full orchestra,
while our parents tangoed into their divorces,
and drank, rejoicing.

The Shower

for Sara and Denise

The chairs are in the round and
we're wearing summer
dresses and earrings, fingers
crooked for tea. Three types
of pregnant teapot, cream cakes
and miniature sandwiches, we're dainty
bulimics in the face of all this
nervous excess, greed and giving,
the unsung chorus of our
dark histories:

adoptionsabortionschildren
nochildrenbychoice
nochildrenandworried
pregnantdoesn'tknowityet
lesbiannotoutoutdoingthe
hokey-kokey. Putting it all off
for another life.

Silver cream jugs, blue
freesias and snowy calla, crystal
vases, so many flowers.
We animate, jingle
with glittery bracelets,
handbag props, costume
jewellery for the occasion.

The gifts are passed round the circle
for us to touch, bless, covet, a
choreography of manners, of

propriety, we stroke the
Peter Rabbit quilt,
catch a nail on the satin,
hold up the tiny booties.
Nobody,
not even the rain,
could have such small feet.

A floor show of wrapping paper,
ruby spools of ribbon. The sash windows
open to the backdrop of a summer city.
The baby
still offstage, curled under the soft wraps
of his mother's floral-print dress,
her face, flushed and smiling,
reflected upside down
in a silver spoon, and,
who knows? Happy.

Mat. Leave

This is a journey
back to the fifties. Spy
on your mother, see her
braced to the yoke of the stroller,
stopping to chat to neighbours
the smiling language of
born-again mothers.

Who does she remind you of,
her mouth, dark with lipstick?

How do you explain the hours spent
watching the serious curve
of your son's back
as he pushes Fisher Price from here
to there? How do you describe
the way his hair grows? And who
would possibly want to hear?

Women come and sit on your sofa,
ankles neatly crossed,
handbags by their feet. You find yourself
not only talking about her new hairstyle
but thinking about it later.

This is what it must have been like,
now you understand.
And she bore it,
she bore *you* for this.
Days, strung together
with cups and saucers
catalogues, phone calls.

The thrilling arrival of the male.
            And women,
in their brief prime,
smiling, smiling.

1980

It is half a lifetime since Alan picked me up
outside my East London art school
and we careened down to Brighton,
tributes to Lennon playing on the radio
of his Deux Cheveux Citroën.

What did we know? Alan
not yet calling himself gay, still a
reporter in those days,
and his girlfriend Phoebe
in that peeling, Georgian, student town
at the edge of the clay-green channel
with its twin piers, one lit up
and blasting cheap music, the other silent

crumbling into the sea.
We went to a toga party,
where drunk, shocked students
trailed white sheets, laurel wreaths
tipped over our eyes, clammy naked arms
holding each other up.
We staggered to Lennon's sarcastic rasping:
Do ya do ya do ya do ya wanna dance?

What did we want? Alan and I both thought
that quiet boy Charlie was beautiful so I
went home with him to get one over Alan
as much as anything.
Charlie, with his curved red lips,
never was a boy so white-
skinned and thin. Charlie,
enough ahead of his time

to use condoms, as if glimpsing
the next decade.

Next morning Alan pulled up
outside Charlie's house and I
jumped in the car, pretending
with my laughter that it was really great
with Charlie, when in fact we had been
two speechless corpses
struggling to rattle.

Alan, Phoebe, Charlie.
I think of you. It is twenty years
since that night of "Imagine" and unravelling sheets.
Our lives. Chronicled
by assassinations.

St. Michael's, Sask.

for Tanis

I love the boy who runs between
and under the spinning rain of the hoses
on the lawn in front of the monastery.
I love the way he leaps—no shirt
(the grass whispering)—stands and arches
his child's brown back, his hands
offered to the sheer fan of water
as it dips and circles him,
fencing a flock, transparent birds,
diamonds.

Today it was hot enough to get heatstroke.
My dusty shoes slapping along the straight
roads that grid fields, oceans
brimming with crickets, mice, snakes,
the long hot breath of summer.
As if it were always like this,
as if the small high clouds
had all the sky in the world.

Now the evening vapour trails
are charmed to a flush
on the long, crouched back of the horizon.
I watch the boy, his flamenco with the spray,
lanterns in strung reflection
cleave the dark, the swinging arc
of rain.

Craven

Radio's on soft and I'm pretending
Tuscany though it's Qu'Appelle,
a rose evening after a bright yellow day.
The folded slopes of the valley we drive through
might be olive groves, biblical and plum-blue,
till we stop in a town called Craven,
and the bar swallows the moon in one.

A dark chamber, windowless and charred,
netted with Molson flags and sports banners,
the men's faces flamed with pool-table shadow
and I am hunched into the pay phone
my ex shouting there've been complaints
from a parent that our four-year-old
told another boy to suck his penis
under the day-care climbing frame.

No one's casting aspersions details are hazy
everyone had their clothes on, not to worry
but they've had to document it.
Speak up I'm in a bar, says the mother
from two thousand miles away,
hand cupped over my ear.

In the truck leaving Craven
I'm squeezed next to a woman who says
she feels like a child between her parents.
I think of the mothers in southern Italy
who comfort their crying newborns
by holding their penises in their mouths
like damp rotini. Imagine my son's

compact, wriggly body tucked between us,
till he sleeps to the sway of the truck

and we drive, good parents,
under the open face of the moon.

June Morning

When we fight
I hear the lurid wails of ambulances
at 7:00 a.m., traffic
like a sea around us.

We live in a city,
big creamy squares of light on the wall.
I'm waiting
for our child to be born.

You're still asleep, your mouth
set like a child's above the sheet.
When you wake,
don't tell me your dreams
with their knives and floods.

I dream about birth,
sanctuary, women
round as urns.

When we fight, I shake.
I feel the weight
of black fruit, its ripe segments
lifting my scalp.

Breathe deeply,
don't panic the baby.
Focus
on the geometry of sunlight.

I am calm.
I am calm.

The neighbours start up
their deep thump of daily funk,
the macho heartbeat
that trembles the house.

You stir.

The Scarf

It was long.
A rich, bloody crimson,
the velvet exaggeratedly lush, soft
as a rabbit's trembling fur,
red as the blood spilt the night
she had screamed out their son.

She always did fall
for the gifts he bought her,
he had a knack
for recognizing weakness.
Knew she could never say *no*
to white lilies,
that she would have to forgive
the fist that held them out.
The old game.

Is it for tying up wrists?
It's long enough.
Or a noose, is it?
A soft leash
for a pampered pet?

A woman could smother
under such a colour—
death by velvet.
Or be mistaken for a priest—
if she wears it,
will he confess to her?

This scarf tags, decorates her
like a parcel,

she spins
as it unwinds.

She wears what he gave her.
It hangs heavy, a red bolt.
She finds it
useful. It warms her.

The Measure

For nine months to be
the hieroglyphics in a file.
To *estimate*, leaf
the book of days
to the night when they forgot
time and from that stewy crucible
calculate the date
when she will be
as round as a number nine.

To *chronicle*,
the body an ordinance
survey map, its hills
thumbprints, radiating outward
from the summit's braided crest.
To eavesdrop the fragile descant
of a heart within a heart. Appraise
the echoes and clicks of ultrasound,
imagine, sound made light!

Admire the snowy image,
the aquatic spine,
as moustached Victorians might
have clustered around
the first swimmy photographs,
chided the child who moved,
the blur
of her ribboned head.

Party, Eight Months

My schoolgirl fears embodied,
the Incredible Hulk, I tower
over normal people,
chest ripping my shirt. Big
but weak—can't open a jar of jam,
can't even tie my shoes.
Panting I'm propped
on the sofa,
a Kafka-esque insect on its back
 (women are the ones
 who change this way).

I'm taken to the film party
and parked by the food,
watch the plum-lipped
slim-hipped women dip
and lean, rubies in their noses.
They flutter and gaze at the big egg
as if it's okay now to stare.
The kind ones ask first
if they can touch, and I know them
by the care in their hands.

I leave before the dancing gets going,
clutch banisters, haul myself
down the steps, past a pack of
smokers, sucking back beer bottles.
They hold in laughter
as I hoist my ungainly self
into a car, which visibly
sinks.

Settler

uninvited you
have made a home in me
sea horse
embedded in this body
I thought was mine alone
with its strong easy lines
its monthly tides

I could pry you
off my walls
send you floating away
with a vague blessing
assume you will come back
on cue

I did not choose you   sea horse,
you chose me
            blue flame
burning small
(steady) in the dark

Bird-Heart

The screen lights up and suddenly
there you are. After months
of dark privacy I get to spy on you,
white cave drawing curled
in your tinsel cradle, bird-heart
tempo twice the speed of mine,
intact, separate, within your
cage of bird-bones.
Blind, not yet a dreamer, you
tolerate my clumsy amazement
with an elegance that
silences me. No one
will take you from me now.
I have carved in your name
and offered it up.
You wait to scan the sky
with the gift of dumb faith.

Boys

It's one of the forty-four reasons for waiting till I'm thirty-three—
because of the fifty-fifty.
And today, on the muffled snow-screen
we believed we saw the *difference*,
tucked between delicately crossed legs, floating, sweetly oblivious
to all this gender chaos out here.

As I write, boy children shout in the street.
They do things I just can't understand,
are truly passionate
about vigorous contact with plastic firearms,
anything even slightly kickable, and later, who guns
a car hardest.

They'll approach each other with puffed chests and crossed arms
and argue the point, their girlfriends tugging at their elbows
saying, *it doesn't really matter, Steven, it doesn't matter.*

Serial killers, pedophiles, and dictators are men, perhaps
I'm growing one inside me. Imagine, *testicles*
like loaded plums, blooming softly
with anger.

And the penis, oh, innocent enough now,
A dreaming chrysalis, a tender fiddlehead,
brought into the world through no fault of its own.
Sacred, harmless as my little finger.

So.
I resolve to cherish this.
As his father must feel, tucking it reverently away,
cupping it from the soccer ball. After all,
he only has one. I have it

safe inside me now, and later, after I've
unwrapped myself—been unwrapped—
handed his body over to the world—*himself to himself*—
    then I will show him another marvellous trick:
    how to grow a woman
    inside a man.

Being in the Water

At the swimming pool
people smile
in that soft, guilty way she's got used to.
The usual struggle to undress—
to unbuckle sandals.

She carries it
like a huge egg in front of her,
walks to the edge,
her gait slow, tentative.
Stands and watches the children's diving competition.
She does not want
to get wet.

But in the water
it's as if she's not pregnant anymore;
suddenly her body
is her own again,
buoyant and quick,
following a lifetime of instruction.

It's as if this were years in the future
and her child is one of the divers,
cutting through the blue air
as she pulls easily
through the water,
carrying the baby under her
like a memory.

Or she'd never met the man
and was still living alone,
the child only a vague idea,
a shapeless wish for another time.

Or perhaps they'd had the abortion, after all,
and she doesn't think about it often.

She finds she's still a strong swimmer—
that hasn't changed,
despite these dense months.
She thinks about teaching her child to swim,
getting him a little orange life jacket
and supporting his thumping ribs
as he splutters and kicks.

She thinks about the time
only weeks away now,
when she'll be one person again,
and she is pricked by nostalgia.

She grips the rail
to haul herself out,
crosses over into gravity again
and resumes her cautious step.

Later she sits on the terrace
with damp hair
and watches the shining backs
of the butterfly stroke.
Watches the children diving,
slicing through the air,
delivered,
for a moment, suspended.

Hands

A light   a spaceship
swaying wildly above

a green-robed chorus around
their reaching hands
the doctor's lips opening   *push* *push*

my mother is there
a hand mirror   I refuse
I grip the birthing bar
scream and bite
it's *good*
to bite down on hospital property
and   I   push   him   out

in the little hand mirror I see
a dark crescent of new wet hair
and everything is suddenly possible

frantic   he's here
lifted onto me as we planned
          completely alive
seal-grey eyes learn my face
with the amazing illusion of wisdom

the nurse has tied her hair back
red ribbon like Christmas
his hands wave   she laughs
calls them big as hams   and I
          mother-protective
decide I

love him
for his startled hands,
cross conductor
reaching for music

he's doing tai-chi
pulling the air aside as if it were weighted
groping for light

he's not doing tai-chi
he wants to feed that's all
stop joking and start being a mother
                    says my mother

he sleeps
hands folded. An old mole
a gentle cleric

my breasts prickle and itch
he'll soon forget
this sign language, this halting tune-up,
          he
          who orchestrates my life.

Two

Night

The neon-lime digits of my clock
flip to two.
Still a baby, this boy
turning and turning,
fingers finely curled
knees bent up plump
and ankles crossed as they were
in the slow sound of rushing
when I, incredibly,
was his round crib.

Perhaps his fetal, starfish hands
reached for shifting light
my slow hands—cloud shadows
passing over him again and again
raspberry stained glass
stroking and guessing...

Three o'clock. He stirs
spins like a cat to standing.
I envy his deep, easy tears
his acceptance of fury.
Fetch him to my tangled bed
my reward
my warm consolation.

The soft grip of his mouth
tugs open again
a grief I have carried all my life.
Rain's low percussion lets this happen
that feminine voice that carries us
through the night.

Simple sedation of milk returns him
to sleep's dark bloom
his whole being ripe and fed.
And in this world are all the safe things
I can surround him with:
his lambskin, blankets
that smell right
humidifier for his breathing.

My wrung-out lonely body
that wills him to sleep, to dream
of floating, of sunlit shapes, hands
passing over safe green water
(*I* am the mother I grieve for
she sits in me tonight).

Morning

It is morning and upstairs
in a room surrounded by silent larches
a woman is getting into bed with a man

he has a cold
the scattering of damp Kleenex and
the red rims of his eyes suggest
that he will not want to make love

which is partly why she's there
she wants his warm morning skin
sweet tea and silence
but no claws
no digging
and pinning
and crying out
she feels as if she will never
want that again

all the exposure
the white lights
the biting down
the nurses shouting   push   push
all the people who saw her
open up
be pulled over to another shore

and now she is taking back
all the times when loved
or unloved
yes or no
her body galloped on without her

Their baby talks to himself in the next room
coos and soft cackles flutter over his crib

women friends told her
her body would change and now
she sees it's not so much
a question of dimension
as attitude

with giving herself over completely
she has completely reclaimed

the man sleeps
his face pale and exposed
in the bright morning room

she is guarding
gathering it up in her new soft flesh
her new tough flesh

she is naming herself
          mother

New Dad

Later, blinkered by daily business, I would forget
your small acts
of tying the strings of his bib,
rubbing his knobbly gums with the
analgesic gel you made runs for,
in the rain, to the all-night drugstore.

We had that child together and,
so consumed by him, I forgot your part in it;
as if I had taken a drug that makes one forget,
awoken in a different country.
Now I see you
with the red and yellow ribbons of the sling
you wore to soothe him—your man's way
of breast-feeding, his sagging body the size
of a bag of flour against your chest,
the beating warmth, the fat of you.

I see the red and yellow cotton strings
tied across your back as you paced the room
that was still our home, the lamplight
winter-strong on the cross
of your harness, so girlish
over your big back, the baby's back
curled into you, his scrawny legs
and dangling red feet, their soles untrod.

You cupped his skull, his cobweb hair,
as if it were water in your palm,
because you were his father and he knew it,
as he knew *my* body. I had forgotten all this, how
we were transfixed by the minutiae of his sneezing,

his bowels, his teeth as they forced their way through.
And I untied you. Loosed you
out into the night to search for another
painkiller, unable to bear it, the intimacy
of that life.

Man

He made love as if he were
born for her body, and she
the perfect element—
carrying him, opening
under him, as if he were a
huge ship—a cruise liner, say,
or a ferry—
launched into her,
unsinkable, strong.

But docked
he becomes shocked,
hunched, shaking
with fear in the sunlight,
            telling her
he is a bird inside—
a seagull perhaps,
or a swift.

Custodians

Into this fierce wind
my child's father is flying
back to Toronto, to his
filthy house in the Portuguese
district, the kitchen floor
too black to walk on without shoes.

Will the plane be delayed?
Power lines down,
leaves and branches shaken
all over the road.

I will cast a storm after that plane.
Kick it on.

I will drive away through the rain
with my son.
A quiet radio,
windscreen wipers erasing
the whispered hiss
of the custody words
back and forth
as our baby sleeps in his seat.

I will ease the car out
onto the highway
and melt in with others, our lights
a slow string through rain.
And if he looks down,
wiping a hole in the mist,
scanning the dark,
he will not find us.

La Pietà

He lies across me, head thrown back,
in his throat a pulse,
a flickering insect inside blue tracery—
reminder of his blood, his body
clean and naked as trust.

There have been so many moments like this,
when I, who have always feared the male body
am holding the bouquet of my life.

I don't want other women to touch him.

Friends help at bath time,
towels across their eager laps,
their soapy reaching hands—
it's all right, *I'll* do that.

I treat him like a little god
and when god shits and pukes
I clean it up and wash his feet.
Which makes *me* god, makes me *good*.
Two gods
alone in a white cell
a-hum with holiness.

3:00 A.M.

she is gathered over him
rustling
unbuttoned

he is curled into her
whorl of hair a thumbprint
starfish fingers gently pulling
the leash he has on her
softest leather

all her losses
cancelled out
filled
by quiet rain
like a woman whispering
through the addictive blue night

her breasts like stars
like birds
that have found their home

Whale Birth, Vancouver Aquarium

The schoolchildren are told how lucky they are,
what they are about to see
they'll remember for the rest of their lives.

The orca, swollen tight as a drum,
her claustrophobic circling of her space.

A chilly day, raining. TV cameras. Waiting.

Then a fin sticks out, a tail,
her frantic swimming, and I double up
in memory of the contractions,
that particular, rearing pain.

The last big push and with a plume of blood it's out—
grey white stripes, perfect miniature design, like a toy—
the calf

sinks. She noses it up,
as if it might have stage fright and need help.
But it sinks
like a bullet,
all its tapered weight pulling downward
through the cloudy water.

The vets say nature
has to take its course.
They leave the dead calf in the tank with the mother
so she can fully grieve.

She tries to teach the new one to jump for the crowd—
till the water grows private with the dark.

Public/Pool

Silently the swimmers
slide in, sink. At home
in water's airless tug, solid
flesh buoyant in saline, the dip and
bulge of arm, wedge
of elbow a shark's fin, and we push

back to the aquatic, at the borderlands
of human, a longing
in the tension between
spirit and the laws of gravity, the suction,
and pushing against life,
and for our lives.

If water is the unconscious, *if*
water is spirit, we (matter)
race against ourselves,
our personal uselessness, or,
(belaboured notion) for its own sake.

Near death's gentle lip, the human suction
tight closed, the sexlessness of it,
beyond gender; and I love
the isolation (I have been accused of this)
the escapism of water, silent but
alongside, *in-element*

but separate.
I have always longed
for that kind of togetherness,
water's glassy barrier, our skin

a tight coat, without puncture.
And the risk always

of blood, pluming into the water, the question
of body as bait.
Length after length we
keep moving, because,
like sharks (gasp
                    of our fish mouths)
                    we must.

Therapy

Just conversation
between free adults in a pact,
choosing to play explorers, she
in a safari hat with a butterfly net,
me in my flippers,
searching for that hidden trail
to the sunken, hanging gardens,
the lost tribe.

I'm the client, the one
who came in out of the rain, sat down.
Penetrating, active
in my diving gear, splashing gamely
back under, flippers waving, eyes wide
under the mask.

Here's a thought:
perhaps there *is* no missing link
and it's absurd, this replay
of a scratched tape,
it was all so long ago, in the
waving fields of childhood. It's science
fiction, it's playing time machines,
bringing the past
into the present this way.

But I believe it, like a round-eyed child.
Let her words tumble over me,
hope that some
will bring me luck.

And we keep company, sip Earl Grey
as the rain types neatly outside,
a couple of eccentric archaeologists—
an expensive
and dubious dig.

Checkup

Autumn, my favourite season,
and the trees outside the cancer clinic
are aging beautifully.
The receptionist is so friendly
and the people in the elevator
joke with us—something about
getting stuck, and who you would
choose to be stuck with.

They call your name
and take you away
to scrutinize your skin;
your arms, behind your knees,
between your toes.
That warm place
at the back of your neck.

I look at the mauve and blue flower prints,
leaf through last month's *Glamour.*
Picture you standing naked
a few rooms away.

I know I should be feeling
something profound—suspect
you brought me along as a favour
to provide material for a poem.
I know that years down the line
I'll understand all this better.

But today, all I can come up with
is how rich and solid the names are
as they're called out.

The people who have lived inside
their names disappear
into examination rooms:
Angus McHenry, Elizabeth Green,
William Rider.
You.

The Convention

for Esta

In our hotel, a baby-shower convention.
Big-bellied girls in smocks and trainers flow
through the main doors.
Many steer wide-eyed toddlers, lug bigger children.
All the impregnate women of Salmon Arm
convening.

And me, hunched in my long coat like a
black crow, towering in the lobby.
"Are you registered?" the organizer inquires.
She has a broken arm.
I hear her repeat the story again and again
of how she fell off a ladder.

Earlier, in the thrift store,
a bearded father's chiding growl
and his sad son. Easy to imagine
that big man roaring, striking out.
His wife, pregnant, too, and silent.
I saw them screech away in a truck,
his finger jabbing the air.

Hey, what do I know.
Perhaps they're all happy, those women,
pink and blue balloons bobbing from their new strollers
and with each other to talk to.

The organizer, her arm healed,
the trucker, cradling his new baby in his big palm.
The son, not sad, watching.

Daddy's Home

and it's birthday wrapping paper
and wrestling and laughing
and sand in your shoes
and a new red bike.
    Who gave you that?
    My daddy.

Daddy's home
and you strut beside him,
a miniature version:
two round faces,
four blue eyes.

Bonsai kid, you
love it when Daddy
makes faces behind teacher's back,
sticks out his tongue *with food on it*,
gets the kids squealing.

You cling to him, push Mummy away,
    go 'way, Mummy.
You are dizzy
with the possibility of a male world,
the relief of switching loyalty,
and you cling to his leg, you cling,
as if that might
make him stay.

Watching *The Lion King*

we like the part when Simba
is a baby and gets lifted
up by the monkey

I used to carry your bum
in one palm
my little loaf
your damp fresh flesh

is it wrong
to want to eat your child?

he is a parcel
a pastry
limbs like raw pulled dough
with their jokey apple muscles

my bodybuilder
my *petit choux*
when I pushed you through
that summer day
you crowned *me*
and all the animals cheered

Trucks

How they have split
the lip of the city, sunk
a dead grey lake into the ground.

Adam pulls me down there every day
shouting, *Truck, truck,*
and we watch them digging:
those yellow diggers
that munch and ponder,
their slow-waving necks
tweaked by a small fat man,
a toy within another toy,
the hero of the toddler.

Adam points, frantic
that I should be
as interested as he
in this big-scale homemaking,
this open-air theatre,
approved by the landlords
of skyscrapers and seagulls.
Men with tortoises on their heads
hold clipboards, stand and watch.
This is *construction,*
and Adam yearns.

In our living room
the trucks line up, plastic
bright as the sun.
I think about painting the walls blue,
cleaning out the cupboards.

What to do
with Adam's baby clothes.
I think about hyacinth bulbs.

Adam shovels broccoli across his plate
and whispers, *Vroom...*

Son

They say
he doesn't look a bit
like me.
They say
he has his father's eyes,
        his uncle's forehead,
        and his grandfather's chin and mouth.
(I'm cleaning up and thanking everyone.)

They say (in consolation),
but you're his anchor,
and I think:
Yeah, rusty,
eaten-up.
The drag
of half-forgotten weight
(but thank you, everybody,
thank you anyway).

You

You were born with a jumping bean inside you
and a complete belief in dancing. Why stand
when you can jig? Why walk upstairs
when you can hop backward?
Why sit on a chair when it can so easily be
a cave, a ship, a car? You

drive me wild with your craving
for cookies for breakfast, popcorn or pudding.
Let me eat cake you beseech
and I say *No, no, no.* I am
one big refusal, I am a wall
to be climbed, to be pushed against,
I am the winter coat to be run from,
its empty, reaching sleeves,
I am the hated legume.

You are the kid in the lineup for the water slide
who is doing the hula-hula, your ear attuned
to irresistible rhythms the rest of us are
deaf to, your cells quivering, alight
with the cha-cha, quick-
step and shimmy, you see all worldly objects
as frames for the climbing, bulky problems
for your muscles to solve,

and they do, they do. Sofa springs rise up in praise,
teachers discuss what's to be done, but you
don't stop, you keep on, because you know music
is in the leaves and in the dust. In the sidewalk cracks
and in the *tap-tap-tap* of your shoe.

Every day
you wake up singing, every day
is Mardi Gras.

Protection

At Planned Parenthood they are busy.
As if I'm a neglected child they put me
in front of a video. Obediently I watch
soft-focus men and women (the Planning Parents)
walk hand in hand through a park.
Clearly they are in love
and discussing their contraceptive choices.

A mollifying male voice explains the ABCs
of human pollination. Music like the sound track
from a soft-porn flick tinkles tinnily as the
girders of the female—an O'Keeffe bull's skull, pink—
gamely withstands the onslaught of hordes
of pesky tadpole invaders who itch to plant
their wriggling flags within its rosy walls.

The nurse is sorry she kept me,
ushers me into another room
where dusty samples are displayed.
It's like meeting the stars after seeing the movie,
and, of course, they are smaller than imagined.
I make my informed choice, and,
pockets full of rubbery loot,
hurry out onto the street where it has
started to pour with rain and me, as usual,
with no umbrella.

Best Friend

She looked like Debbie Harry
and we all wanted to dance
the way she danced.
She was the first girl in our class
to wear a bra. She was my best friend.
Totally different shapes, together
we were a blinding combination.
Our thumbs, bitten and painted,
tickets to anywhere.
We liked juggernauts the best, galleons,
shuddering and hissing to a halt,
we ran, jubilant, to its kindly flank
to climb the stairway to trucker heaven,
and somehow we were protected,
they were all benign. We could look down
on family cars as we careered along the motorway,
spinning lies that were sparklingly obvious—
perhaps God is a truck driver
who likes a laugh.
She
was the Queen of Allure,
she even made my father nervous.
Black eyeliner and plenty of it,
brown lipstick, a hex that could not fail.
Our school marks descended as we
skipped class for the playground and swings, singing
"Goodbye Yellow Brick Road" and "Sorrow."
The great smell of Brut still takes me back
to Tony's sofa, his downy upper lip and
stripy tank top, love bites like a tom cat's
paw prints. I didn't know
what a Bohemian Rhapsody was but I kissed him

as if practising resuscitation,
I kissed him as if inventing Third World irrigation,
I kissed off my childhood.
And she,
on a different sofa, with a different boy, did the same,
but we really
only loved each other.
We spent a summer at the fun fairs,
drank Tia Maria under the stars and laughed,
a long way from home.
We did not consult maps,
we knew this would not last,
we had not yet been hurt.
And now she's got a daughter and a mortgage
and I haven't seen her dance for years.
When I go home, after a year of sketchy postcards,
she lectures me
about getting a foot on the property ladder
and I say,
I know, I know, I know,
        but I just can't bring myself
        to do it.

Christmas

That year I had a camera stolen
on a train to Brighton while I dozed
on and off, as you do, in trains,
in the winter sun.

Yes, I remember the man
opposite me (I told police),
his beard, his watchful eyes.
How he vanished into the crowd
with my new camera,
a present from my father.

What can you expect if you mix
with the criminal classes?
my father said
when I confessed it.
But I was sorry about the roll of film.

That was fifteen years ago.
The boy I didn't marry
standing in the snow, smiling,
arms outstretched, as if to say,
all this, this snow, this land,
these arms, are yours.

We took photographs of the snow,
its waves and drifts. Shadows
of thin trees, and one
of our single bulky shadow
against the bright white,
twin heads linked,

just kids
with a new camera.

And the man who stole it?
God knows, he would have
ripped out the film and chucked it—
the pictures from that dazzling morning
undeveloped and dark.

Dowry

You are the ghostly buffalo   carved in the wall of the cave
your ear to the drip   of the underground streams
your delicate hoof raised in running

You are the rocks   that hold
the pools of quiet sea that stayed behind
arranging and tending   miniature gardens
while the wrestling waves turn back
                        on the rope of the tide
You
are the deep crack in the cliff that
the hunter falls into   never to be found

You wait in the hills for the coal mines to reach you
and lead you   blind   to the family
You fill the house with the hot pungency of rivers   of swamps
At dawn the women lift you
                                cool and soft
and place you in the garden
                to sleep with the bones of the animals

You   are the tree that my mother wrapped her arms around
                the woods
                where the neighbours' children
picked the bluebells
that my father arranged in a milk jug
next to her bed
                that April morning

Break

You still limp from the soccer accident
that met with you at twelve,
your leg stiff in its white cast, bright and chalky
on the sidelines of a green turf.

Perhaps that marked the end of the worst of it,
gave me a summer to run from you
and you time to hobble
into black hallucinating adolescence,
when anger was pulled into lungs
instead of out on me.

Our combat changed then,
you became cool,
with your incense and your Sergeant Pepper coat,
and I became cool, too, something
your stoned friends would giggle about,

the sister. I learned
a passive twisted power.
It seems greedy and chaotic now,
bulimic, the feeding and erasing.
Mechanical, I needed turnover,
as if to keep my metal, clean, oiled—
shark, I could not stop
mowing my way through them.

And every one of them
was you, the friction, the wrestling.
I wanted to hurt, push
into those boys, as if

one can find a peace through chaos,
as if one can be purified in the scrum.

Now I see you old,
your face stitched with lines
against the sun's glare. I
have fought you again and again,
brother. I have wanted to break,
send you sprawling,
then offer you my hand,
taunt you, tend you in the mud.

Greenham

(for the women who participated in the peace protest at Greenham Common Nuclear Air Base, England)

We called to each other
across the wet foggy fields,
a warning, an off-key howl,
or was it grief?

Women stayed for months,
sitting around fires, our tents
stretched over bending branches,
dripping plastic, mugs hanging.
Mud.
          The shape
          of one another's backs.
Silence.

Then the calls, the singing.
A strange sound it must have been,
a lamenting,
as sharp-nosed fighter jets
ripped back and forth
across the gold-streaked sky.

It made the TV news
that a woman had a baby
in one of the tents, a boy.
He was passed around,
wrapped in coats,
held sleeping by the fire at night
while the military rumbled in
and out of the air base,

the American soldiers at ease
with the quiet army
of women around the fence.

The boy will be seventeen by now.
He won't remember Greenham—
though there may be photos:
smiling muddy faces, grown similar,
the black raised arms of trees.

But clear as birdcall
it will be in him,
the lament
that welcomed him in.

Three

Wreck

He starts phoning her
from ridiculous places:
The Golf Club, the skating rink,
the Superstore.
Overwhelmed by the suburban tackiness
of this behaviour,
he crouches under the pay phone
analyzing his many layers of guilt,
one arm flung over his face
against the yellow and white lights,
while shopping carts brim over
with children and groceries
            and sail on.

Charmer

You are too good at this, this
sleight of hand. You ping-pong between,
hold up little mirrors, produce trinkets,
distract us, make us laugh.
We both know
you're a ham, an illusionist
in a shiny cape sewn up by your mother,
a battered top hat and nothing
up this sleeve, nothing up that.
You slip potions into our drinks.
I see you do it, but I'm too
far gone to care. I like being a fetish.

In a puff of blue smoke
lovely assistant number one vanishes.
Where could she be?
I cough till I cry, flap my arms,
wear short, sparkly dresses,
trust you when you say
you can cut me in half.
I let you.

Drum roll, she...levitates!
She is still whole!
Baubles of thin glass
dance and weave over my body.
Deftly, you catch each one
and announce you can absolutely
and without doubt
see the future.

Ativan

he offers her Ativan
says *let it dissolve under the tongue*
and it works she sleeps
hardly registers the front door closing

this is the sleep she longed for
those broken nights when the children were small
she sleeps under a spell
and the children sleep too
the house becalmed as snow falls
dissolving on the black river

she dreams he's driving
across a bridge snow under streetlights
he's walking up an alley hunched into the shedding night
big footprints quickly filled

a candle-lit room patterned with great
bending shadows magic
-lantern cinema on the walls and ceiling he

feeds sushi into her accepting mouth
opens the curtains they watch the snow fall
jazz whispers from the late-night radio

his drowning breath on her breasts
clothes trampled roses the bed a twist of white flags

He slips off his shoes
glides through the house

silent as ether
the children breathe evenly
stretched out as he
left them

his wife
dead still

in the morning she is refreshed
calls it the best sleep she's had for years
they romp in the snow with the kids

It turns out half her friends take Ativan
let it snow *let it snow* *let it snow*

Lice

Jealousy is not green
jealousy is plum-coloured
and mostly mental.
Safe sex? No such thing.
Even fantasy is unsafe.
Dark imaginings. Teeth.
Foam. Erotica. Images
you thought could never
threaten you, never prod
that dark place,
a plum inside.

Limbs heavy
with something that
could be flu, could be
longing, dull and vertiginous.
At home, shaking,
the wife-at-risk, you
carefully pick lice
from your son's scalp,
holding his head
in a good light,
just so.

Mid-Wife

I hauled you naked
straight from another
woman's body. You were
driven, greedy, led
by the begging heart-
shaped head of your cock,
the soft, hanging fruit-brain
of your testicles.
And in the blood-red of candles
we lay, tangled, dazed survivors
thrown from a burning plane. I
pulled you out, you had only
gasping seconds of air, it was icy
and I couldn't bear
to see you shiver, I took pity.
Wrapped you into the warm.
But you're too big now, baby,
you're kicking and I need air too,
I need to push.

Mirror, Mirror

Yes, I'm bored
with the flat prison of my mirror,
that silver lie
that I trust and mistrust.
I don't care
that we are equally in love
with our reflections as with each other;
tonight I *want* to look.
I want to admire
the amber sand dunes
braided together,
the dark drawn-out line
that runs between them,
living strata,
layered one on one,
where they join,
where they part. Oh,
how I love me
(and you're a big part of that).

Graft

If I could have you in this poem I would,
here before me,
quiet, breathing, your face
cold from the night.

I would lead my hand under your coat
to check your heart is still there
and presuming it is
pull your shirt up and reach under
to startle your skin with my fingers.

Now, I want you lying on my red sheets
waiting in your grown body
awkward in your size, aching
from all that exercise you put yourself through.
Darling, you're marvellous, but I want more,

to reach through the gates of muscle and armour,
let me through   to the boy, to the
girl, and back farther,
I will lift the mask and kiss you
whoever you are.
I will straddle you, quick, let's see if the soul exists,
don't you wonder what medals
what roses could bloom?
It will be *release*, a short exhalation of fear,
the curtain's sudden flutter of spirits
clamouring to be let in.

Rise up before me, lay your hands on my head,
absolve me as you promised.
Mail me your fingers—I will not bite them,

I will keep them carefully in my mouth,
I will climb you barefoot until I can see for miles,
I will engrave each of my possible names
on your shoulders,
and later, when we wash them away,
we can admire the faint script of scars
and the blind courage it took
to win them.

Kiss

I had been kissing you
for so long

with words measured
eyes dark with truth

with fingers my hand
casual on your arm

staying away

while pulled by the current
my returning

and lately gratefully
with my body
leaning into you
our gallop of heartbeats

your hands pressed my back
hard
as if relieving pain

and by the time
eventually
our mouths
find each other—

brushing past hair
neck cheek arriving
at the line the centre
of our circling

pause

our breath rising like conscience:
          —this is significance
          —this is the first time
          we are crossing that line
          our awareness parallel
          our mouths dry

both analyzing the thing to death
awkward as parents
holding a newborn
          and as terrified
wanting it   for so long
wanting
just
          to kiss well

Loose

I was testing, as if
tonguing a tooth,
liking the gritty,
guilty sway
as I worried you loose.

I had presumed you
bolted in.
Long-forged.
I had not expected you
to chip, come apart,

the taste of blood in my throat
as you lie in this
curious child's palm
and say,

I'm yours,
keep me.

When You Leave

When you pass over into sleep
you leave suddenly—too soon,,
and you become an animal
I don't recognize.
The bulk of you,
your long legs braided with mine,
your feet like the feet
of a Roman statue,
solid, oversized, beautiful,
as if you had never
worn shoes.

Your rusty breath changes
from quick
to lazy,
deep, steady,
and you are gone, unjoined,
like a ship that had been in harbour,
and is suddenly on the horizon.

There is a nonchalance
with which you do not warn me,
with which you do not say goodbye.

You go to a hot, dry place
where they are all men,
speaking the *real language* of men.
If I had packed a bag for you,
you would toss it away,
lighten your load.
Neither kind nor unkind,
you would not remember me.

The compact engine of
your greedy, healthy breath draws up
all the air in the room; I am
afraid of it,
its confident rhythm
that does not look back,
is gathered in its own sensual oblivion,
and leaves me fretting
on the other side of the door.

Awake I contain you, am comfort.
The truth is you don't need anyone.

Take me with you,
show me how to sleep this way,
how to push off with naked ease
into those waters.
Teach me to fill my lungs
and drink the blackness.
Let me be unjoined,
with you.

A Shell Box

I

The verdict of twin lines bloomed rosy pink,
a cycle of the moon gone missing
and breasts glow,
swollen cartoons.

Hunger like wild fire.
It's in me, it's in me.
Germination, I am
burning with it,
it is in my
clumsy hands.

Little fern, little flame, I *know* you,
I know
what you do to a life.
Spreading till you fill up all the space,
till you suck up all the air in the room.

Start so small, an *idea,* a *so-called* life,
then you capsize the one
who carries you.

Forgive me if you misunderstood,
if we seduced you
onto our chaotic shore.
Believe me when I tell you
there is no home here.

Listen,
sac of my gestation,

immaculate and mistimed,
you took the wrong turn
into the cul-de-sac of my body
and I will turn you back

II

Soberly and reverently we
sit in the doctor's office like churchgoers,
we are gathered together in this place
man and nonwife.
We repeat *I do,*
I do want this.
I sign my name, and he signs
as witness where God is not.

I try potions, needles, but the pea is not dislodged,
the pea clings.
The ultrasound shows two peas.
Comma-shaped smudges
facing each other in yin-yang
reflection.

Not the delicate white cave drawings of *feti,*
not these two, five weeks into evolution.
Prints of our two thumbs.
Our woven DNA
poised to hijack my life.

Miracles?
Two sickle moons. (Nail clippings.)
Only one moon missed,
a cold February moon.

He gasped into my neck
as he left his mark and
life begins
at conception.

This is true; it is not; it is language
man-made
to shame and frighten us.

It is myth.
It is our dumb primitive bodies
telling us their only truth.

III

I have a born son. A lock
of his blond hair lies curled
in a shell box on my desk. To it
I add a speckled pebble from the beach
and a garnet off a broken necklace.

These two glittering impossibilities,
sacrificed
for our selfish, embryonic love
that has already burned down so much.

Brief thoughts
of how we might combine:
my dark hair, his blue eyes.

The two commas
in my womb will never meet, never be
the strangely close friends
that twins can be.

And for that I grieve. I grieve.

IV

In the operating room
awaits the altar of gynecology,
framed by a tableau of women.

I am fully awake,
my eyes are open
as they were that day I first
walked toward him
confident as an athlete
who knows she is ready.

Now my legs are open
in the V of examination,
a lamp interrogates their fulcrum.

I flinch.
Fall apart.
He sits by my head,
we grip hands, I cry
and mewl into his neck.

I have heard this high animal sound before,
so has he, but this is not
a birthing scene, this echo, this
inversion of birth.

Nothing will keep us together,
my lover, my twin.

Sweet smell of female blood.
Blood of my blood.
He looks at what is spilt,

at our nondelivery.
I cannot.

My uterus protests at the pulling away,
the separation.

I am body,
I am mined.

V

An old lady,
I am led to the recovery room.
There was so much noise and now
there is silence.

I lie on the soft bed
with a pure white blanket over me,
a rich invalid on a cruise.

And here you come with a cup of tea
Wreathed in steam.

It is a chilly day,
the dark sea choppy.

I am on the shady side of the deck
where few venture.

I lie
still, stare
at the empty horizon.

Rain, Jericho

Quiet days at last.
We are hiding out here
in this house by the beach.
We have landed, exhausted,
and we have locked the door.

We lie together and
tell each other stories.
We believe we have found home
here, we have grown dreamy,
unreliable, do not
return calls.

Childhood homes: The *swish*
of poplars in Saskatchewan,
the hedges and potholed lanes of Kent.

At night we open
the bedroom window
and listen to the improvised chant
of rain in the trees.

The garden drinks,
its dark earth quiet.

We want only to be home.
A sanctuary of thick walls
around us. The holy,
healing song of the trees.

Privet

Some mornings I walk the extra block
to avoid the house where my son
stays with his father
and sometimes I walk deliberately
past the tall hedges, looking up
at the top-floor windows, the small square
with the safety bars I insisted he install,
the blue blanket he nailed up as a curtain.

I stand behind the thick privet, its dark wall
hung with dewy webs, the FOR RENT sign.
How little we own. My child lies in that
top-floor room and I can't
reach him, can't ease myself
alongside his warm sleep to breathe
the damp yeasty signature
only a parent can love.

I stand here as a woman with
no child, between those worlds.
Tied to his life yet also free of it,
a stranger looking up at a house.
He is not *my* child, but *a* child,
and I walk on to my office job,
my smart shoes clicking.

The Dress

It's been years now and still
she hasn't finished
with grief's long gestation.
Her body fooled but not fooled
by the phantoms it carries, the ghosts
that live in the mother-fat.

She grows. In her mirror's
dusty profile she looks, oh,
five, six months gone, and still
she chooses butter, cream,
as if under siege and
having to lay down stores,
her body the living engine,
root source for another.

She squeezes into the wedding dress
she bought in a reckless fit.
Now it's tight to bursting,
she will be shoved, bloated,
down the aisle, trussed up in ivory.

There is excess in nature.
Animals know it.
Vines, roses.
It is necessary to prune.
Tie the blind kittens
in the chloroform bag.
She remembers
her father doing that,
the hanging bundle, his grip.

She is grieving nothing. Buds
spoiled by frost, sliced from their root
by a good gardener.

Three Years Deep

in the dream of mothering   her body speaking
the soft language of hands   hips curved

not for eyes but to carry   speaking
the early language of *bloom*   *spread*   *kick*
wipe   as she changed species   the baby

a hard peach   felling her to the floor in a green
flapping gown   the sudden batter
that neither gas nor oxygen could balm

nurses carried away silver kidney dishes
sloshing with port-blood   the lamp
a drunken eye careening over her as she

gave up all modesty and split her skin
into a new country where her body
was peasant   shrouded
where it had displayed

now she would walk
invisible to men and be happy
relieved of the trussed corset of the feminine

no longer the younger sister using
frippery as currency   walking in a hungry body

now she *was food* and she fed herself
full-fat   a revolving refectory

her child's soft hair and skin   the only perfume
she needs

In Another Life

She carries phantoms,
    two halves.
And sometimes she believes
she is still carrying them,
those princes in the tower.
    They are alive
    tipped against each other
    in fitted symmetry—
    peach halves in a jar.
And she's huge,
wading next to him through fallen leaves.
Proud, humiliated,
their lives abdicated
    or only beginning.

But she's flat. Scooped.
She has lain on the mountainside and
asked the birds to take her eggs, leave her
empty. She has given away her jewels.

            The self-help book says her grief
is abnormal, that she should seek professional help,
but what's to be done?
Both extraordinary and banal, this story
of their DNA; the minute specifications
of what might have been.

Friends. Trying for years.
They cannot conceive of this.
She could have handed them over:
            gorgeous dishes.

But there is evidence:
a doctor's scribble
filed in a clinic, testament
to a successful procedure,
while outside grandmothers stroll
murmuring prayers.

The rain goes on,
and the days.
            They have been to the moon
            and there was nothing there.

February

A deadly month, February.
This year I paint a chair green,
a chair for our table.

For we have built a home here,
pushed choices aside like cards.
These, not these.

February is succulent, exhausting.

Birds build and the music of trees
is an overture, a rough tuning.

I plant tulips, hyacinths, watch
for their folded hands.
The big breath of white cherry.

Was it here last year? This wet green world?

Today my lover buys me two roses, red
as artificial blood. Their buds tight
but forced. No scent to breathe.

I should go back to the recovery room,
something did not   work right
there, before.

I look at the five stones on my ring:
one for my son, two
for my borrowed children
and the others: dark
sapphires, small memorial fires.

Oh, the empty luxury
of writing this. I have tried
to name it
beautiful.

Housework

This morning the children are at gymnastics,
ballet, sleepovers, and the house
is an empty city, pillaged and burnt.

Batman and Mr. Freeze lie facedown,
exhausted lovers. Early drafts of poems
now are overlaid with alphabet hieroglyphics,
lush red crayon, rows of A's
that radiate out to a wail.

Across the bay, snow gathers for winter.
            The pale sea, cold as the sea
that argues against the jagged island
where I lived for thirty years
and is now a shape, pea-green and tiny
on my sons' junior globe.

Look, there it is.
And all that blue is the ocean.

I tidy the strewn drawings,
find a shoe box bed for the action heroes.
Slide open the doors to the garden,
its carpet of red leaves.
            In England
my mother would have made a bonfire,
pitched them on, wiping her eyes. Here,
            I don't know where they go.

Shift

slowly gradually

it occurred to her
the body was not to blame

that what felt ruined
and for years *had* been
a broken-down house—

its doors pried open
its windows smashed—

had grown soft green

forgiveness had settled itself
moved in

and in the woods
there is breath
the sound of running water

stillness

Eating the Earth

I want to lie flat on my parents' lawn and rub the warm grass
against my cheek   breathe it
I want to cover their property
with the weight of my body so that I know it

can't move   the sun will watch   I will eat into the earth with
strong jaws I have seen naked urban warriors do this
mining tunnels that snake under endangered parks   I will

crawl under the surface   there will be giant molehills
I will have huge mole hands
the house will tilt collapse   I will eat it too
I will have it all
I will eat the antique furniture and yes I will eat my parents

Or perhaps I will keep them in my breast pocket
tiny legs kicking   squeaky voices protesting
Shh I say   it's the only way

I will live fugitive and hide all over Britain   camouflaged
in my tweed jacket on the moors   against the bracken   the heather
lie and watch   the silver jets crisscross the sky   the earth
is as round as the moon

I will take my child with me too   he would want to be there
There's room in my jacket   I can button him in tight
I will feed him worms   renew lactation   find shelter
under a wall   not a wall around a house

a wall trickling through a northern field
stones bigger than heads   like bonbons   like kitten's grey wool

the shifting   the grouch of such a wall
and the delicacy

Were they to come for us I would walk into a river
the silky water
We wouldn't drown   I would fashion reeds   pipes
to breathe through
Wait   wide-eyed   lean
against the current

One night I will find my way home   to the condemned site
I will live there   decorate
the earth walls with snakeskin and leftover silver

And when they have forgotten the family   I will surface
up to the wild garden of hollyhocks and deranged roses
We will play hide-and-seek   my child and I

Oh   I will be buried there   the earth
will be rich with bone

MIRANDA PEARSON was born in England and moved to Canada in 1991. She received an M.F.A. in creative writing from the University of British Columbia, where she was poetry editor for *Prism international.* She has taught at Simon Fraser University and currently teaches in the University of British Columbia's Department of Creative Writing. Her poems have appeared in numerous journals. She lives in Vancouver.